CLASSIC ROCK RIFFS
OVER 40 ESSENTIAL CLASSICS

T0055361

PLAYBACK+
Speed • Pitch • Balance • Loop

To access audio visit:
www.halleonard.com/mylibrary
Enter Code
5147-3027-3952-2363

ISBN: 978-0-7390-8588-2

Visit Hal Leonard Online at
www.halleonard.com

Contact Us:
Hal Leonard
7777 West Bluemound Road
Milwaukee, WI 53213
Email: info@halleonard.com

In Europe contact:
Hal Leonard Europe Limited
Distribution Centre, Newmarket Road
Bury St Edmunds, Suffolk, IP33 3YB
Email: info@halleonardeurope.com

In Australia contact:
Hal Leonard Australia Pty. Ltd.
4 Lentara Court
Cheltenham, Victoria, 3192 Australia
Email: info@halleonard.com.au

ARTIST INDEX

Artist   **Page**

CONTENTS

25 OR 6 TO 4
by CHICAGO

Words and Music by
ROBERT LAMM

The title of Chicago's second Top 10 single, "25 or 6 to 4," refers to the pre-dawn time when Robert Lamm was attempting to write a song about the songwriting process.

The guitar player on this track was the late, great Terry Kath. Terry was a big man with a big voice and an aggressive playing style. We suggest you attack this riff with all downstrokes.

AIN'T TALKIN' 'BOUT LOVE RIFF
by VAN HALEN

Words and Music by
EDWARD VAN HALEN, ALEX VAN HALEN,
MICHAEL ANTHONY and DAVID LEE ROTH

*To match recording, tune down a 1/2 step.

Moderately ♩ = 138

*Recording sounds a half step lower than written.

Van Halen erupted on the rock scene with their debut album in 1978 and almost singlehandedly brought hot guitar playing back in vogue. Their signature spandex wear and exaggerated hair set the stage for the '80s "Hair Band" era. "Ain't Talkin' 'Bout Love" uses the simplest arpeggios played with a typical EVH flourishes of palm muting and artificial harmonics to make a rock statement with aplomb.

GAIN　BASS　MIDDLE　TREBLE　PRESENCE　VOLUME

6

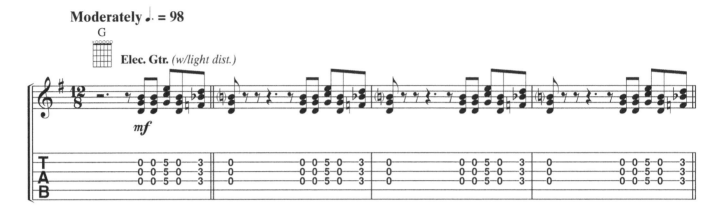

BAD TO THE BONE *RIFF*
by GEORGE THOROGOOD
& THE DESTROYERS

Words and Music by
GEORGE THOROGOOD

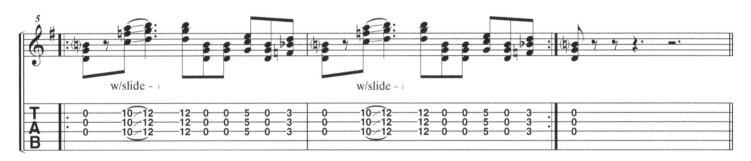

George Thorogood & the Destroyer's 1982 hit "Bad to the Bone" has become the proletariat rockers' signature song. George usually plays with a slide and in Open G tuning. When playing guitar with a slide, it's important to keep the slide parallel and directly over the fret wire to sound in tune. Check out "Manish Boy" by Muddy Watyers to hear a precursor to this riff.

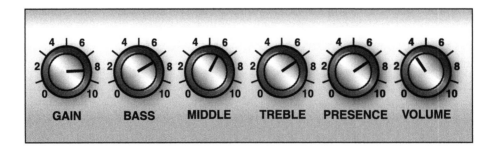

BEAT IT

by MICHAEL JACKSON

Written and Composed by
MICHAEL JACKSON

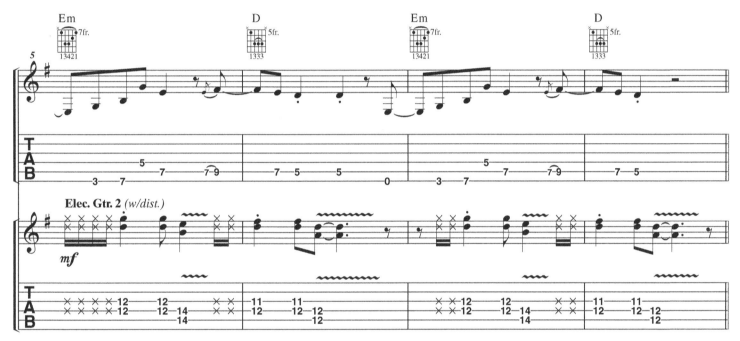

Michael Jackson's 1983 smash hit "Beat It" is primarily known among guitar players for the ripping Eddie Van Halen solo but we've got to give props to studio players Paul Jackson, Jr. and Steve Lukather who laid down the killer riff that makes the song. Beware the tendency to begin the riff on the downbeat. It actually starts on a pickup note on the "and" of beat 4.

Elec. Gtr. 1

Elec. Gtr. 2

BLACK DOG RIFF
by LED ZEPPELIN

Words and Music by
JIMMY PAGE, ROBERT PLANT
and JOHN PAUL JONES

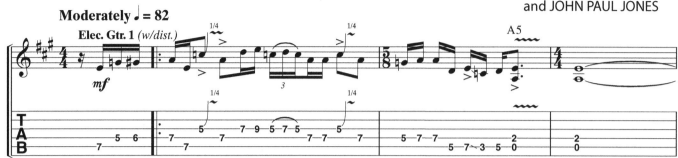

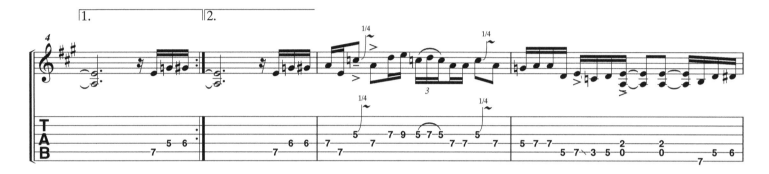

Chorus:

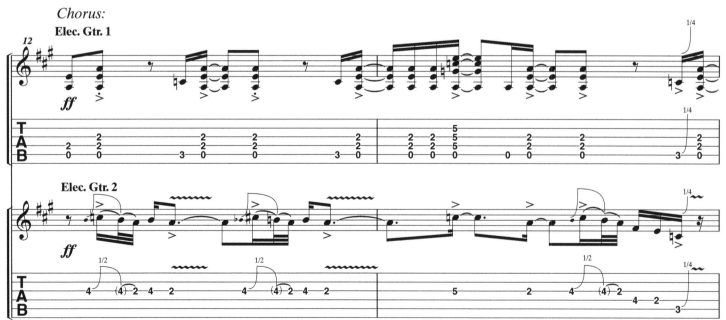

Elec. Gtrs. 1 & 2

Jimmy Page, Led Zeppelin's guitar player, has revealed the secret to the buzzsaw guitar sound featured on "Black Dog." He says he plugged his Gibson Les Paul into a direct box into a microphone preamp of the mixing console with two compressors in series to get the distortion. Then each line was triple tracked to build up a sound that resembles an analog synthesizer.

Listen for the drum stick click on the downbeat to cue the guitar before the first 16th note in each phrase. In measures 9–11, note how the B note on the 7th fret of the 6th string that begins each iteration of the B riff keeps shifting. On the first occurrence, it's played with a downstroke on the "and" of 2. It next comes in with an upstroke on the "e" of beat 4, followed by a downstroke on beat 3.

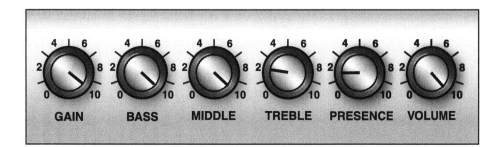

CHINA GROVE *RIFF*
by THE DOOBIE BROTHERS

Words and Music by
TOM JOHNSTON

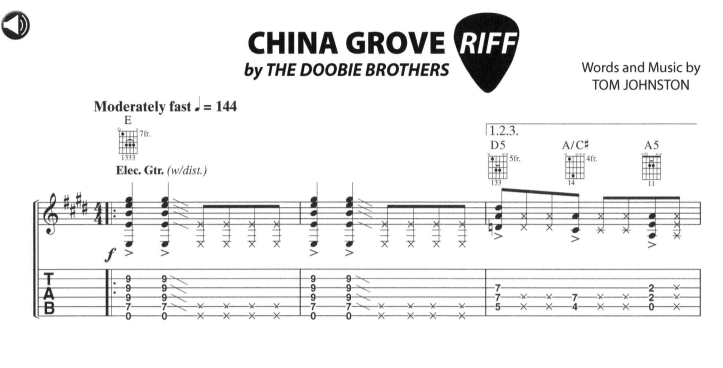

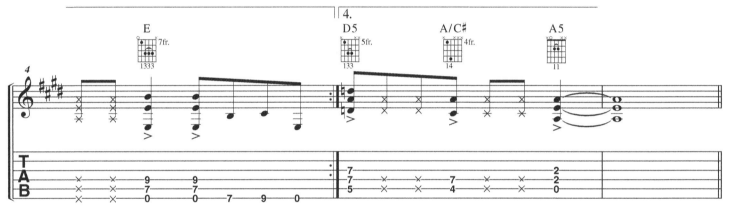

The riff for "China Grove" is built around mostly standard barre chord shapes, with the exception of the two-note A/C♯ chord that requires a bit of a stretch between the index finger and pinkie. The key technique you'll need to play the riff is fret-hand muting. Indicated by x's in the standard notation and tablature, fret-hand muting involves loosening your grip on the strings so that they are no longer touching the frets, effectively preventing them from ringing when strummed and "choking" the sound so that only a hollow, "chick" sound results. Strum the two E chords at the seventh fret with accented downstrokes and be sure to use down-up strumming for the eighth-note rhythms.

DOMINO RIFF
by VAN MORRISON

Words and Music by
VAN MORRISON

Moderately fast ♩ = 130

Elec. Gtr. *(clean-tone)*

"Domino" is a song that Van Morrison had in his pocket for a couple of years before he finally put it out in 1970. Good thing he waited because it became Morrison's highest charting single (even topping "Brown Eyed Girl").

The light but infectious electric guitar riff on Morrison's joyful R&B paen to radio was played by session musician John Platania. It's a classic example of the clean out-of-phase sound of the combination of bridge and middle pickups on a Fender Stratocaster. Note how Platania masterfully exploited various inversions of A and D chords and the 9th fret, the 5th fret, and the 2nd fret to make the most out just those two chords.

GAIN   BASS   MIDDLE   TREBLE   PRESENCE   VOLUME

DO YOU FEEL LIKE WE DO *RIFF*

by PETER FRAMPTON

Words and Music by
PETER FRAMPTON, JOHN SIOMOS,
RICK WILLIS and MICK GALLAGHER

*Implied harmony.

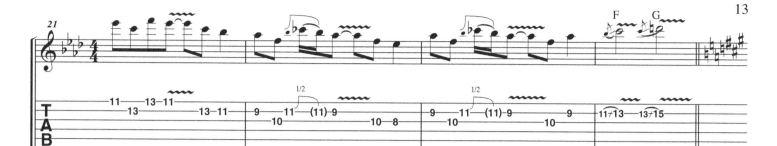

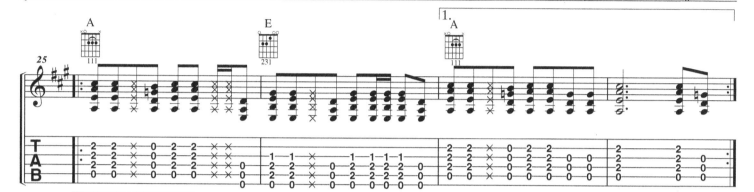

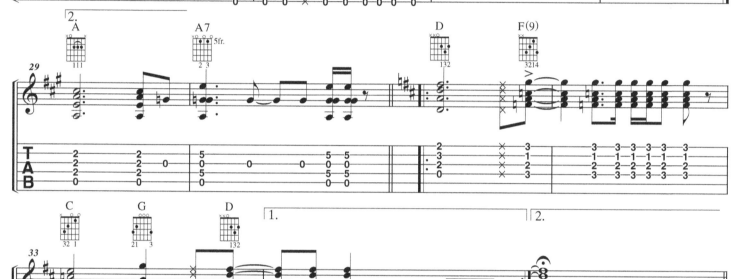

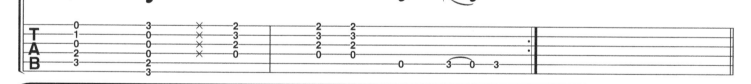

There are a few albums that define an era. Almost every young person alive in the mid-seventies seemed to have a copy of Peter Frampton's hugely successful *Frampton Comes Alive*. A highlight of that double album and Frampton's concerts for more than 35 years has always been his extended rendition of "Do You Feel Like We Do."

Rather than just the intro riff, we're giving you the whole guitar part up through the first chorus. Note the modulation from the key of D minor to F minor in measure 17, the change to A major at the Verse in measure 25, and one more change to D major at the Chorus in measure 33. Astute listeners will note the introduction of a fast rotating speaker effect between measures 16 and 20.

DON'T STOP BELIEVIN' RIFF
by JOURNEY

Words and Music by
JONATHAN CAIN, NEAL SCHON
and STEVE PERRY

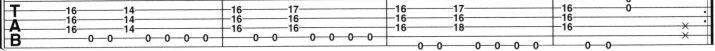

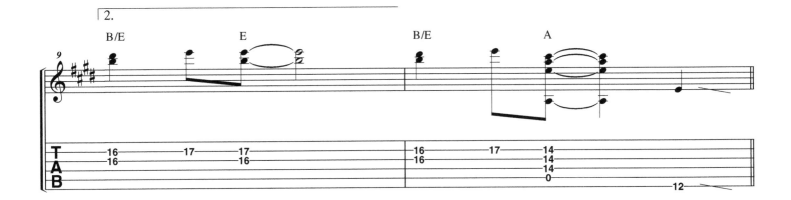

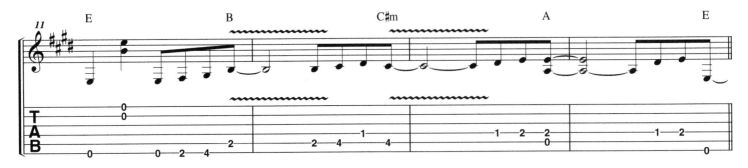

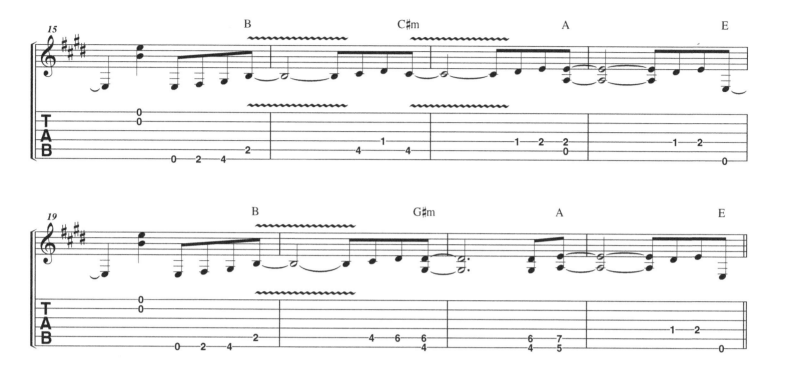

Journey's axeman, Neal Schon, created the instantly identifiable riff for "Don't Stop Believin'" and that song's attitude has sustained the band through more than three decades filled with personnel changes.

Be mindful of palm-muting the open-string pedal tones during the "street light people" part and have fun with the step-wise passing tones between chords during the verse riff.

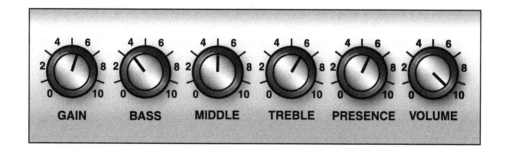

GLORIA RIFF
by THEM

Words and Music by
VAN MORRISON

Penned by a young Van Morrison, "Gloria"'s simple three-chord progression and crowd-pleasing chorus has been a staple of garage bands and proto-punks since it was first released by Morrison's band, Them, in 1964. It subsequently became a Top 10 hit again in 1966 when the song was covered by Shadows of Knight.

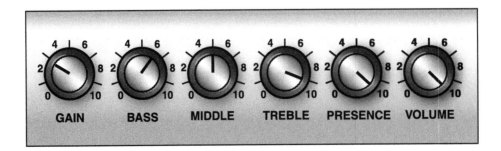

GOOD LOVIN' GONE BAD RIFF
by BAD COMPANY

Words and Music by
MICK RALPHS

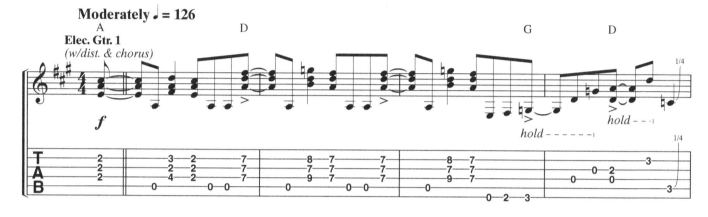

Bad Company's bluesy guitar-driven records were extremely popular in the '70s. The riff for "Good Lovin' Gone Bad" shows how a simple well-executed guitar part can be a serious earworm. The key to playing this riff is to barre your index finger across the 4th, 3rd, and 2nd strings, leaving the 5th string open and be prepared to add the 2nd and 3rd fingers on the 2nd and 4th strings respectively. Be prepared to slide quickly from the 2nd fret on the A chord up to the 7th fret for the D chord.

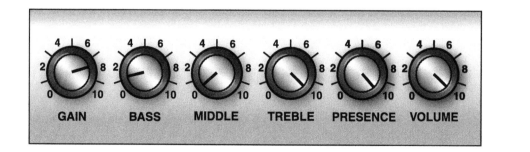

HAD TO CRY TODAY
by BLIND FAITH

Words and Music by
STEVE WINWOOD

Short-lived supergroup Blind Faith made an indelible mark on rock history with their lone album. "Had to Cry Today" featured the interplay of two fine guitarists, Eric Clapton and Steve Winwood. Clapton begins the riff, based on a G minor pentatonic scale and Winwood joins in later with a harmony part. Winwood's part is mostly the interval of a 5th above Clapton's notes but, because he also sticks with the pentatonic scale, the harmony above Clapton's D note turns out to be a B♭, a 6th.

IN THE MIDNIGHT HOUR RIFF
by WILSON PICKETT

Words by WILSON PICKETT
Music by STEVE CROPPER

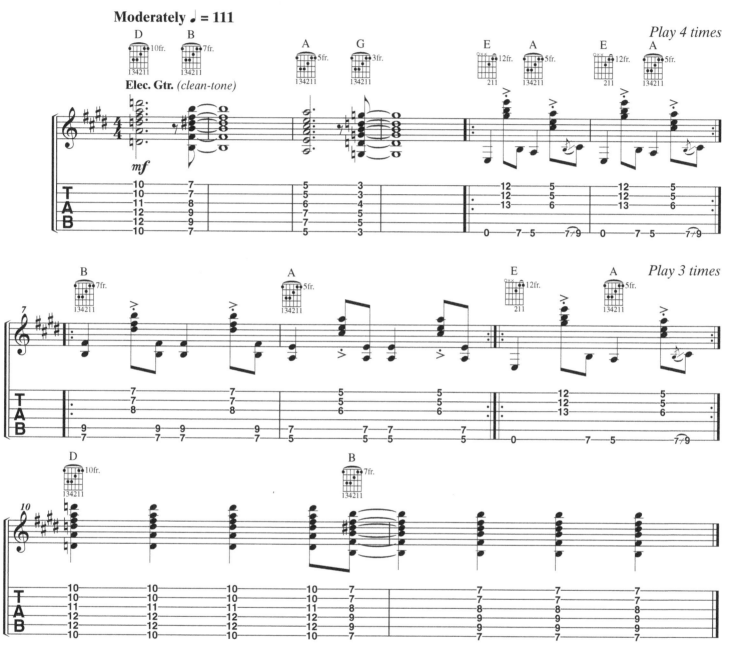

The introduction of "In the Midnight Hour" features what guitarist/songwriter Steve Cropper calls a "money lick." By the second chord, everybody knows what song it is. It was so effective that, less than a year later, Cropper recycled the same chord progression in reverse ("retrograde" for the music theorists) for the intro of Eddie Floyd's "Knock on Wood."

I DON'T NEED NO DOCTOR RIFF
by HUMBLE PIE

Words and Music by
NICKOLAS ASHFORD, VALERIE SIMPSON
and JOSIE ARMSTEAD

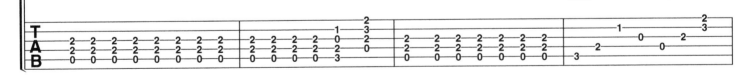

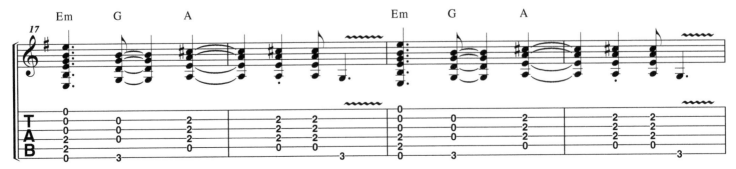

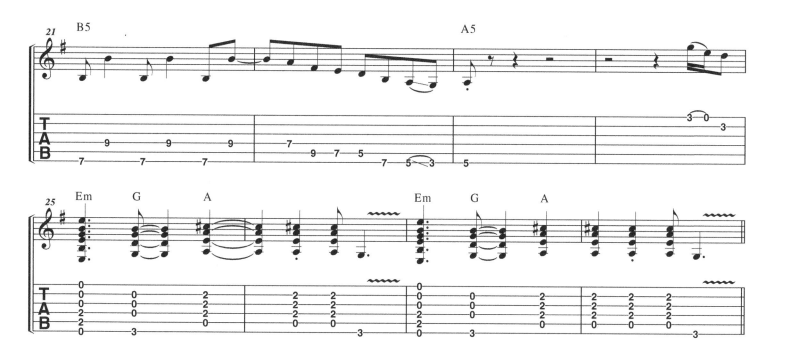

In 1971, Humble Pie took a swinging bluesy Ray Charles tune and transformed it into an out-and-out stadium rocker. To play this song, crank up your amp and hit your guitar hard. If you're not sweating by the time you reach the first verse, you're not playing hard enough.

IN-A-GADDA-DA-VIDA

by IRON BUTTERFLY

Words and Music by
DOUG INGLE

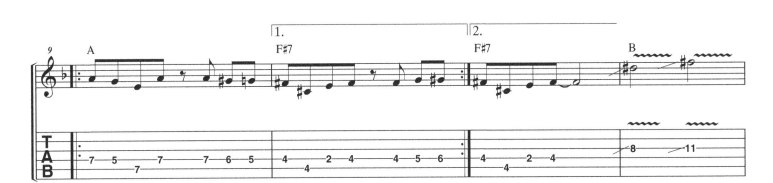

Every Clearasil-using kid with a guitar in 1969 had to play "In-a-Gadda-da-Vida"—along with bell bottom trousers and a peace sign necklace, learning this hypnotic riff was de rigueur for the era. In case you missed the dawning of the age of Aquarius, here's your chance to turn on the fuzz pedal and fire up the lava lamp. Groovy!

JAMES BOND THEME *RIFF*
by JOHN BARRY ORCHESTRA

Music by
MONTY NORMAN

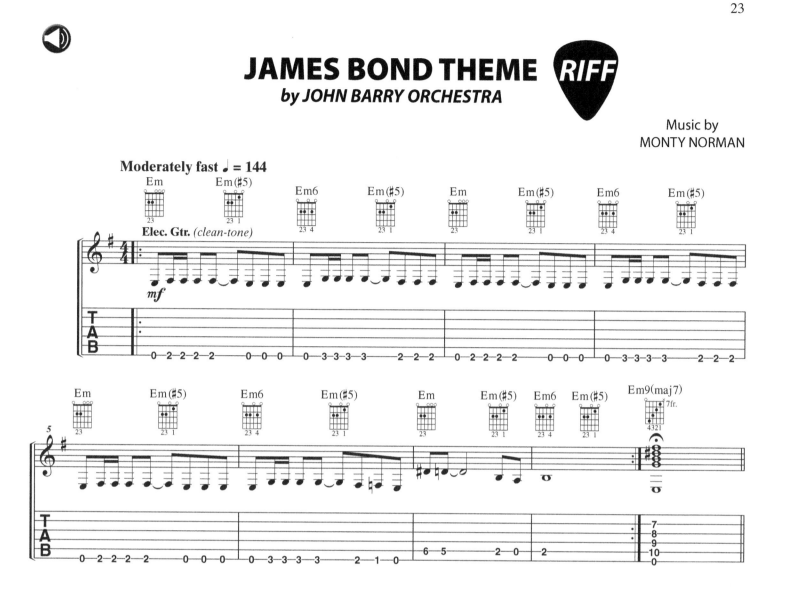

The "James Bond Theme" has been heard in 22 James Bond films and countless tributes and parodies. The riff was originally recorded by British session guitarist Vic Flick playing an archtop acoustic guitar with a clip-on pickup through a Vox AC15 amplifier. Quite a different rig than the usual surf guitar music it was designed to emulate. Never mind, the sound of that motif and the ultra-cool ending chord forever established the sophisticated yet dangerous genre of "spy" music.

JUMPIN' JACK FLASH RIFF
by THE ROLLING STONES

Words and Music by
MICK JAGGER and KEITH RICHARDS

"Jumpin' Jack Flash" has been covered by a variety of guitar players who have adapted it to their own style. Heck, even Keith Richards himself has performed the song in both standard tuning and in Open G tuning with a capo on the 4th fret. Here we present the riff the way it was originally written and recorded—in Open E tuning. Of special interest is the method Keith produced the overdrive heard on the record; he deliberately overloaded the input of a primitive cassette tape recorder with an acoustic guitar. Richards employed the same effect on "Street Fighting Man."

The key to playing the tricky E5 chords in the Acous. Gtr. 2 part (as on beat 1 in measures 2, 4, and 6) is to lift the 2nd finger from the barre on the preceding B5 chord and lay it lightly across the 2nd and 3rd strings.

KASHMIR RIFF
by LED ZEPPELIN

Words and Music by
JIMMY PAGE, ROBERT PLANT
and JOHN BONHAM

Guitar in DADGAD tuning:
⑥ = D ③ = G
⑤ = A ② = A
④ = D ① = D

Moderately slow ♩ = 80
Intro:

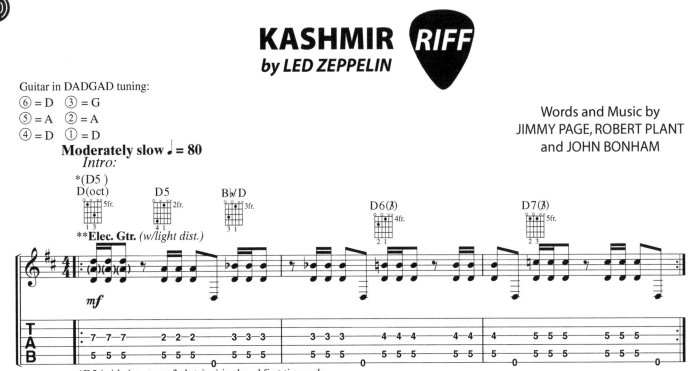

*D5 (with A note on 3rd string) is played first time only.
**4th string is muted with left hand fingers while playing this figure.

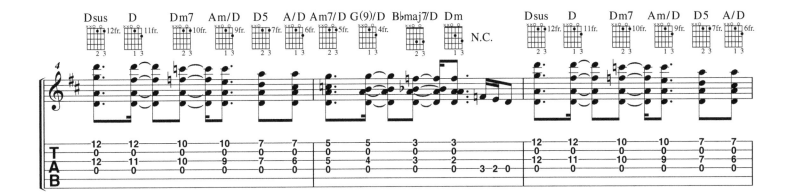

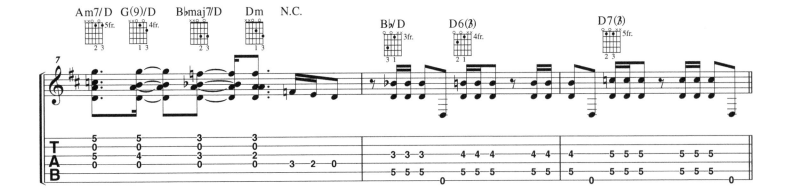

The DADGAD guitar tuning inspired Jimmy Page to create the ersatz Middle Eastern riff that pervades Led Zeppelin's "Kashmir" like the scent of patchouli in a hippie pad. It's a simple riff with an ascending chromatic line on the 3rd string against a pedal tone D note on the 5th fret of the 5th string. The notes for the descending chord progression beginning in measure 4 may look intimidating but a quick look at the chord frames reveals that it's a simple sequence of two alternating chord shapes along with some open strings. Be careful to allow the open 2nd string to continue to ring on each chord.

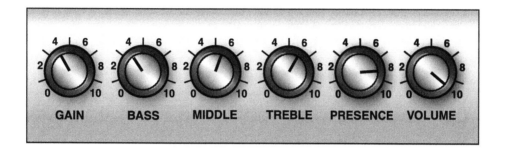

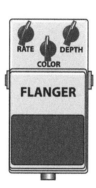

LAYLA
by DEREK & THE DOMINOS

RIFF

Words and Music by
ERIC CLAPTON
and JIM GORDON

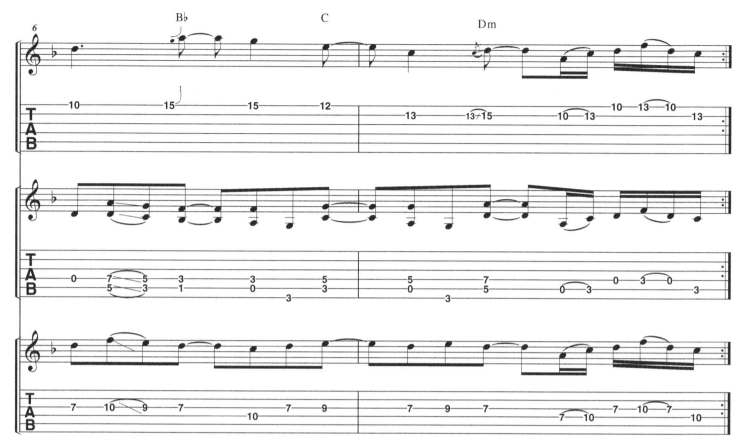

The melodic element of the fiery signature riff to "Layla" was inspired by the vocal melody of an Albert King song "As the Years Go Passing By." Guitarists Eric Clapton and Duane Allman masterfully overlaid multiple guitars, beginning the riff in three different octaves and fleshing out the harmonic progression with harmonies rather than block chords.
This riff was recorded with tiny Fender Champ tube amplifiers so resist the temptation to apply too much distortion to your guitar.

Elec. Gtrs. 1 & 2

Elec. Gtr. 3

LE FREAK RIFF
by CHIC

Words and Music by
BERNARD EDWARDS
and NILE RODGERS

Moderate disco beat ♩ = 118

Nile Rodgers created the riff for Chic's "Le Freak," a song that's always guaranteed to fill the dance floor. Rodgers' funky technique involves deft coordination of the two hands with muted strings and allowing only selected notes from each chord to sound. Leave your index finger barred across the 5th fret, loosely strum in a continuous 16th-note rhythm, and keep the fretted notes staccato and you'll be halfway there. Use the TNT software to start with a slow tempo and gradually build up speed until you can match the original tempo.

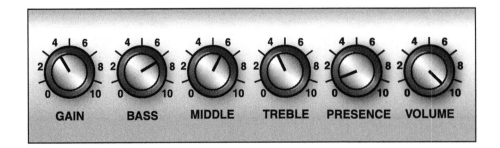

LIFE IN THE FAST LANE
by EAGLES

Words and Music by
DON HENLEY, GLENN FREY
and JOE WALSH

The genesis of "Life in the Fast Lane" was Eagles guitar player Joe Walsh jamming a spontaneous riff at a pre-concert soundcheck. Glen Frey recognized a good hook when he heard one and told Walsh, "Keep that, it's a song."

The trickiest part of playing this riff is the way the phrase begins on the downbeat of 1 the first three times but, on the fourth time, it's anticipated on the and of beat 4 in measure 3. Just a little speed bump in the fast lane.

LOLA RIFF
by THE KINKS

Words and Music by
RAY DAVIES

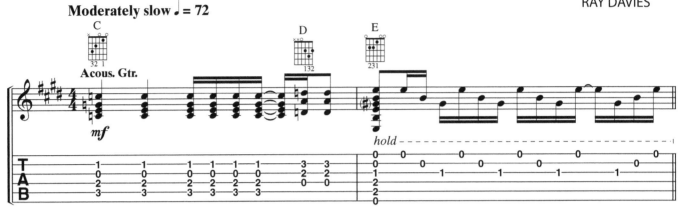

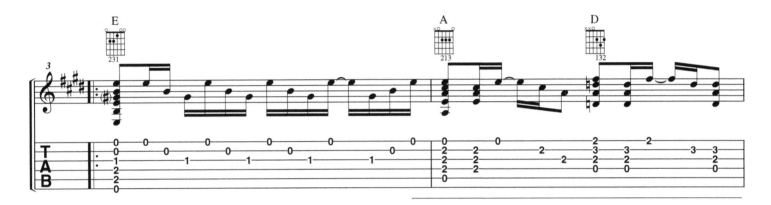

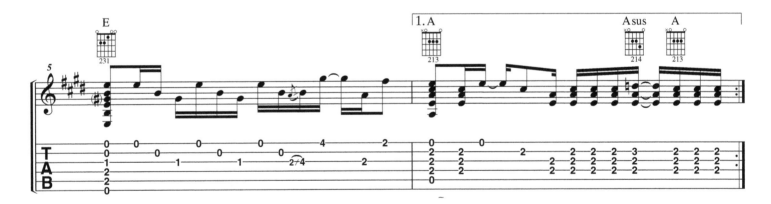

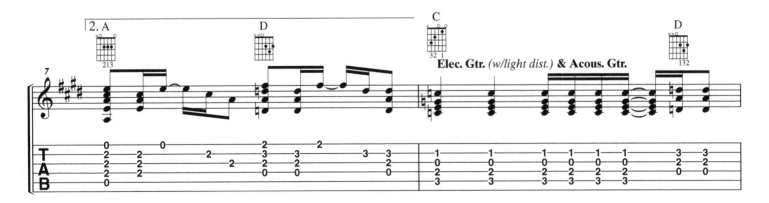

33

The ringing chords of Ray Davies' resonator guitar launches rock's most popular ode to transvestites—the Kink's "Lola" from 1970. Brother Dave Davies kicks in with a tasty major pentatonic lick on his electric guitar in measure 9.

LIMELIGHT RIFF
by RUSH

Words by
NEIL PEART

Music by
GEDDY LEE and ALEX LIFESON
Play 3 times

"Limelight" has remained one of the most popular songs by the Canadian trio Rush for more than 30 years. The lyrics reflect drummer Neil Peart's long-standing uneasy relationship with fame. The music shifts time signatures continuously from 4/4 to 7/4 to 6/4 back to 7/4 and 4/4. No need to busy yourself counting all of those different meters, once you're familiar with the song, so long as you don't lose the quarter-note pulse, you'll do just fine.

MONEY RIFF
by PINK FLOYD

Words and Music by
ROGER WATERS

Moderately ♩ = 119 (♫=♪♪)

Play 4 times

Selling more than 200 million albums, Pink Floyd is one of the most successful rock bands in history but, ironically, "Money" has the distinction of being one of only two Top 20 singles the group ever released.

Roger Waters' acoustic demo recording of the song reveals he had the song's shifting time signatures of 7/4 to 4/4 to 6/4 and back to 7/4 right from the git go. Guitarist David Gilmour's contribution included the orchestrated second and third electric guitars.

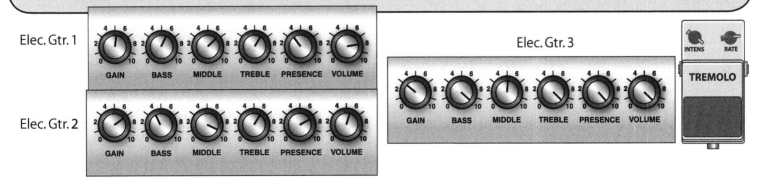

MOBY DICK · RIFF
by LED ZEPPELIN

Music by
JOHN BONHAM, JOHN PAUL JONES
and JIMMY PAGE

Drop D tuning:
⑥ = D

Moderately ♩ = 94
*D

*Chords are implied.

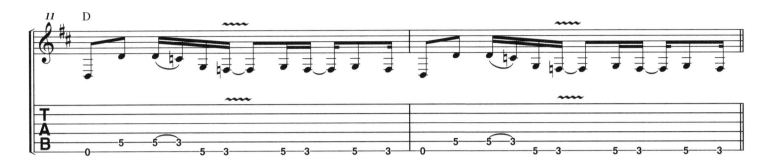

Named for Herman Melville's mythical leviathan, "Moby Dick" is Led Zeppelin's adaptation of the riff from Bobby Parker's "Watch Your Step" into an extended John Bonham drum solo, sometimes as long as 30 minutes.

Using Drop D tuning, Jimmy Page and John Paul Jones double the riff through a standard 12-bar I–IV–V progression in the key of D.

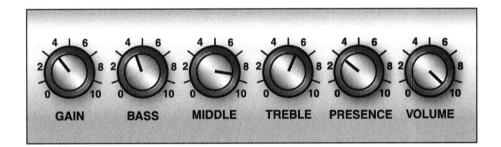

THE ONE I LOVE RIFF
by R.E.M.

Words and Music by
WILLIAM BERRY, PETER BUCK,
MICHAEL MILLS and MICHAEL STIPE

"The One I Love" is from R.E.M.'s fifth studio album and was their first record to crack the Top Ten. In the key of E minor, guitarist Peter Buck uses the guitar's open strings to maximum advantage.

RUNNIN' WITH THE DEVIL RIFF
by VAN HALEN

Words and Music by
EDWARD VAN HALEN, ALEX VAN HALEN,
MICHAEL ANTHONY and DAVID LEE ROTH

*To match record key, tune guitar down one half step.

Moderately ♩ = 96

*Recording sounds a half step lower than written.

"Runnin' with the Devil," from Van Halen's eponymous debut album in 1978, is a prime example of the band's early combination of Eddie Van Halen's brown sound and David Lee Roth's swagger.

This song is tuned down one half step. Using the pitch change feature of the TNT software you can play the song without tuning down. When playing this riff, be mindful of the alternating dynamics in the verse (beginning in measure 3). Start off balls-to-the-wall but prepared to quickly notch it down with a softer touch.

GAIN   BASS   MIDDLE   TREBLE   PRESENCE   VOLUME

BOOST   BRIGHT

TREBLE BOOST

PANAMA *RIFF*
by VAN HALEN

Words and Music by
EDWARD VAN HALEN, ALEX VAN HALEN,
MICHAEL ANTHONY and DAVID LEE ROTH

*To match record key, tune guitar down one half step.

Moderate rock ♩ = 141

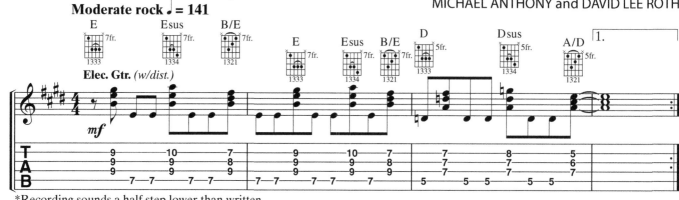

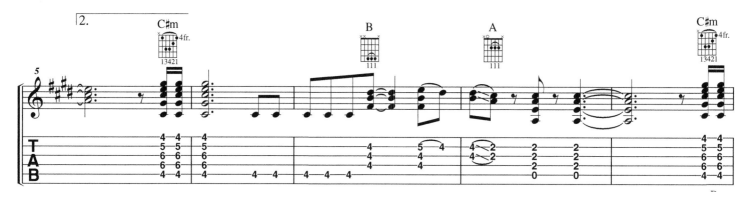

*Recording sounds a half step lower than written.

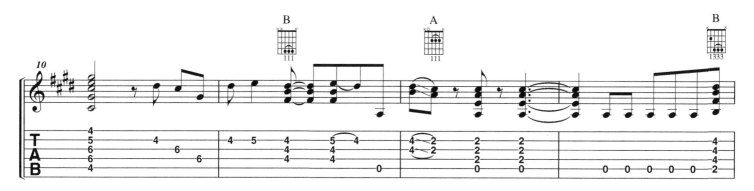

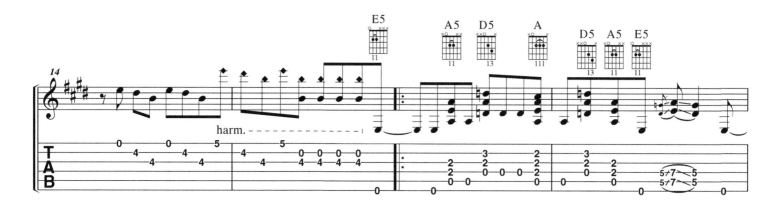

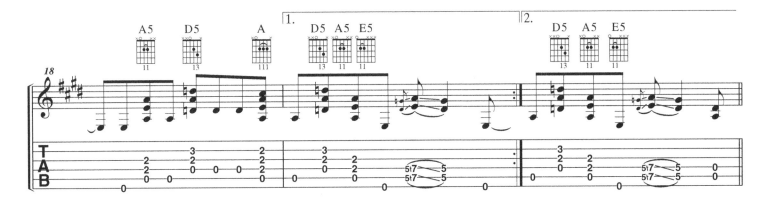

"Panama" is a Van Halen hit from 1984 (the year and the album) named for David Lee Roth's 1969 Opel Kadett car.

This song is tuned down one half step. Using the pitch change feature of the TNT software you can play the song without tuning down. Don't miss the switch from fretted notes to harmonics at the end of measure 14.

PARANOID RIFF
by BLACK SABBATH

Words and Music by
FRANK IOMMI, JOHN OSBOURNE,
WILLIAM WARD and TERENCE BUTLER

Moderately fast ♩ = 156

Intro:
Band enter 3rd time

Play 4 times

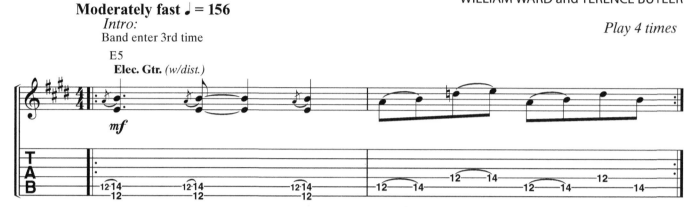

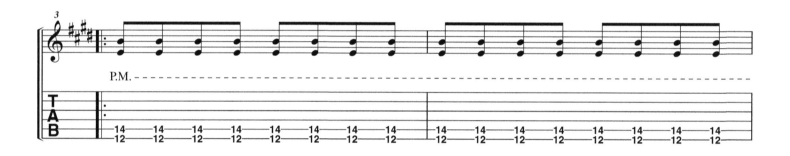

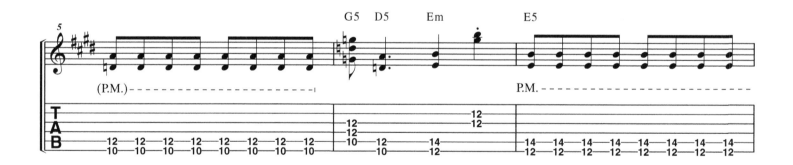

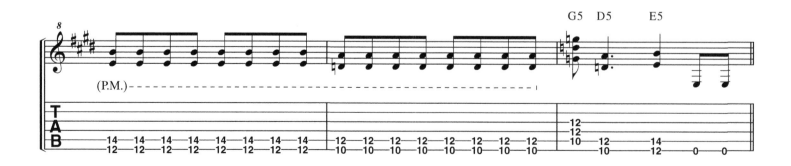

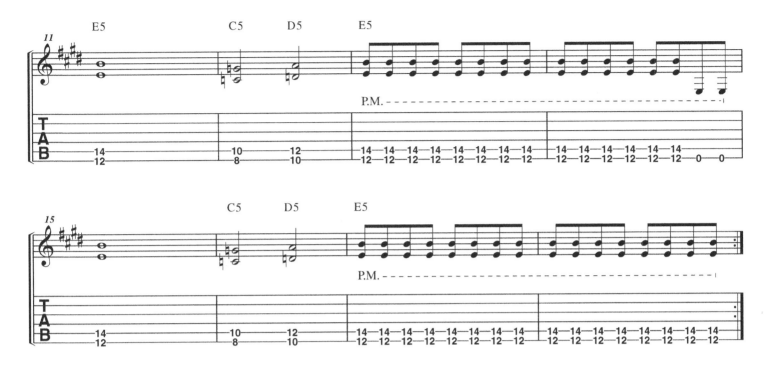

Clocking in at less than three minutes, the frenetic title song from Black Sabbath's second album, "Paranoid," is both quintessential heavy metal and proto-punk. The chugging riff was played by guitarist Tony Iommi primarily on the 6th and 5th strings. Attack the fuzz-drenched rapid-fire eighth notes with all downstrokes.

(I CAN'T GET NO) SATISFACTION RIFF
by THE ROLLING STONES

Words and Music by
MICK JAGGER and KEITH RICHARDS

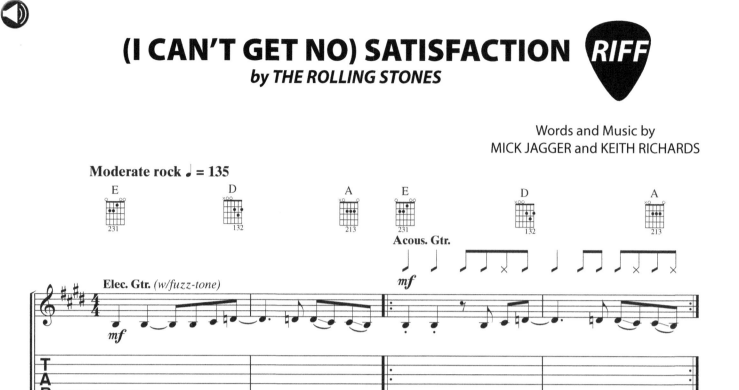

Consistently voted as "the greatest guitar riff of all time," Keith Richards groggily sang this melodic fragment into an early cassette recorder one morning just before falling asleep in a Clearwater, Florida motel. The fuzz-drenched three notes that kick off "(I Can't Get No) Satisfaction" can legitimately be called the fountainhead of all subsequent rock guitar riffs. Ironically, the guitar riff heard on the record was only intended as a guide for what Richards intended to be a saxophone part but the Rolling Stones' record company rush released the song before the horns could be added.

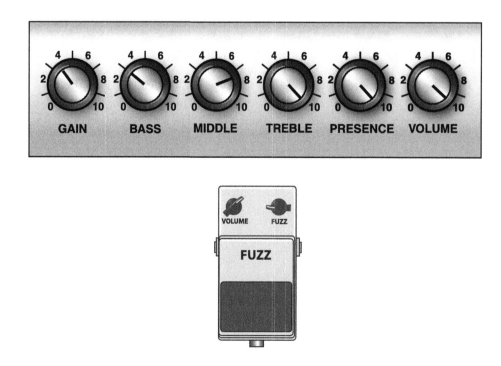

SING A SIMPLE SONG RIFF
by SLY & THE FAMILY STONE

Words and Music by
SYLVESTER STEWART

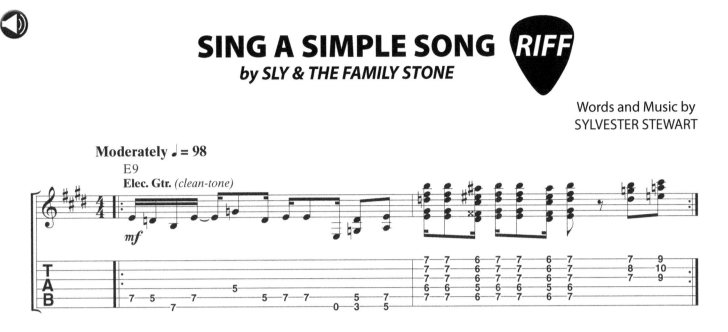

"Sing a Simple Song" is, hands down, one of the baddest riffs ever. The tune has been covered and sampled by numerous R&B artists since its original release in 1968. Jimi Hendrix and Band of Gypsys directly quoted the riff in their own "We Gotta Live Together" in 1970.

On Sly & the Family Stone's original, the two eighth note chords on beat 4 of the second measure are played by the horns. We've taken the liberty of making a composite arrangement to complete the riff. Similar to the funky riff in "Le Freak," keep your picking hand loose and fret the notes slightly staccato.

SOUL MAN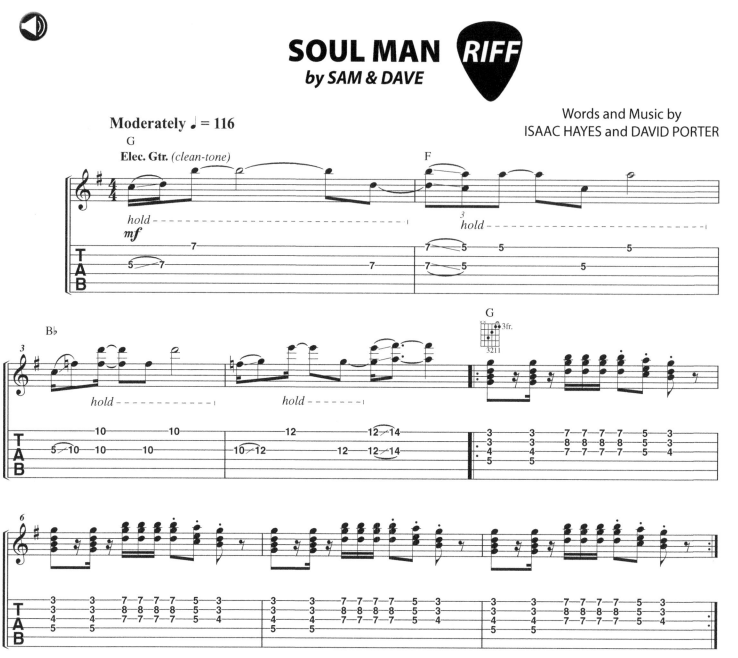

by SAM & DAVE

Words and Music by
ISAAC HAYES and DAVID PORTER

"Soul Man" exemplifies Steve Cropper's restrained and tasteful approach to creating a guitar part that is both memorable and integral to the song. It begins with some soulful sixth intervals that outline the suggested chords in the intro followed simply but effectively with embellished G chord inversions in the verse.

SPIRIT IN THE SKY RIFF
by NORMAN GREENBAUM

Words and Music by
NORMAN GREENBAUM

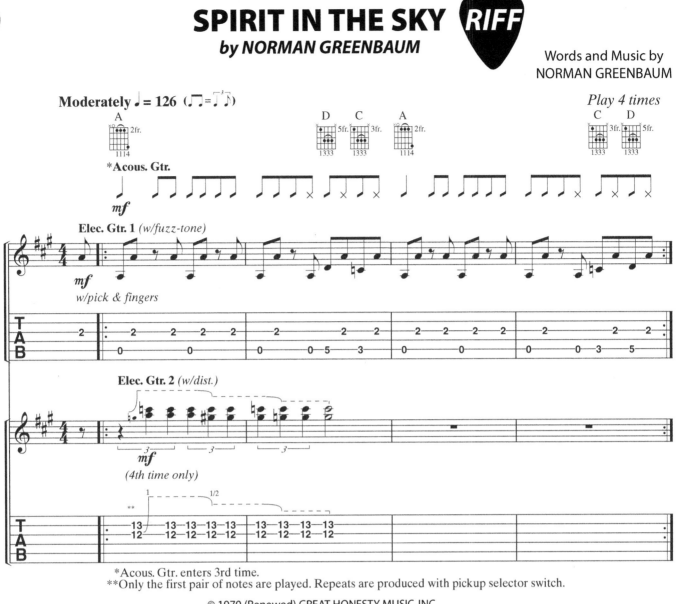

*Acous. Gtr. enters 3rd time.
**Only the first pair of notes are played. Repeats are produced with pickup selector switch.

Norman Greenbaum biggest hit came as the result of seeing Porter Wagoner on TV singing a gospel song. The recording for "Spirit in the Sky" features Norman playing the main riff with a Fender Telecaster thru a fuzz effect and second guitarist Russell DeShiell playing an SG/Les Paul thru a Marshall Plexi and an overdrive pedal. DeShiell has explained how he played the intriguing "beep beep" guitar parts. On a two-pickup guitar with individual volume controls, set the bridge pickup volume to zero and the neck pickup volume to max. Set the pickup selector switch in the middle position and, just before the beat you want the notes to enter, bend and pick the first two strings as shown in the TAB. Flick the pickup selector switch from middle to bridge in the quarter-note triplet rhythm you want the notes to sound while gradually releasing the string bends.

Elec. Gtr. 1

GAIN   BASS   MIDDLE   TREBLE   PRESENCE   VOLUME

FUZZ

Elec. Gtr. 2

GAIN   BASS   MIDDLE   TREBLE   PRESENCE   VOLUME

DISTORTION

THE SPIRIT OF RADIO

by RUSH

Words by
NEIL PEART

Music by
GEDDY LEE and ALEX LIFESON

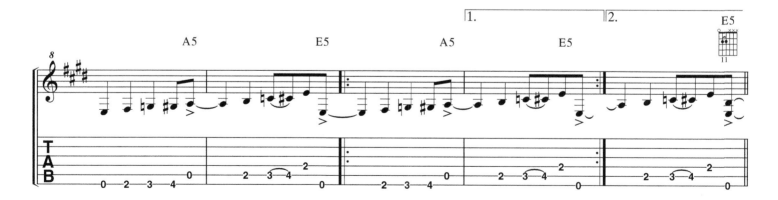

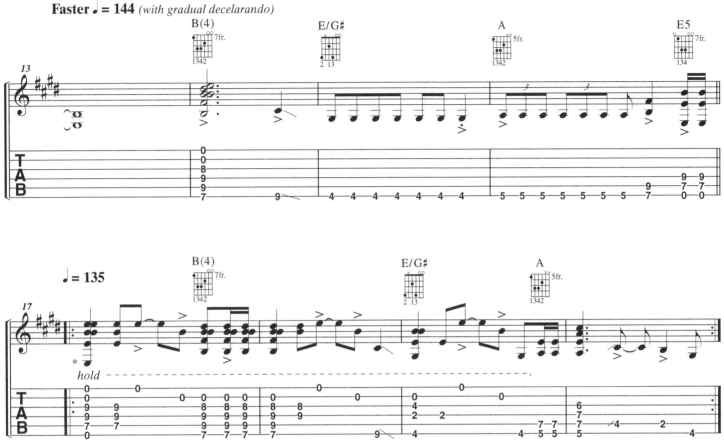

*Open 6th string E note only on beat 1 on repeat.

One of the most popular songs from Rush's 1980 album *Permanent Waves*, "The Spirit of Radio" begins with a rapid flourish of pull-offs. Watch for the tempo changes in measures 13 and 17.

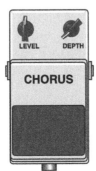

STAY WITH ME **RIFF**
by FACES

Words and Music by
RON WOOD and ROD STEWART

Open E tuning:
⑥ = E   ③ = G♯
⑤ = B   ② = B
④ = E   ① = E

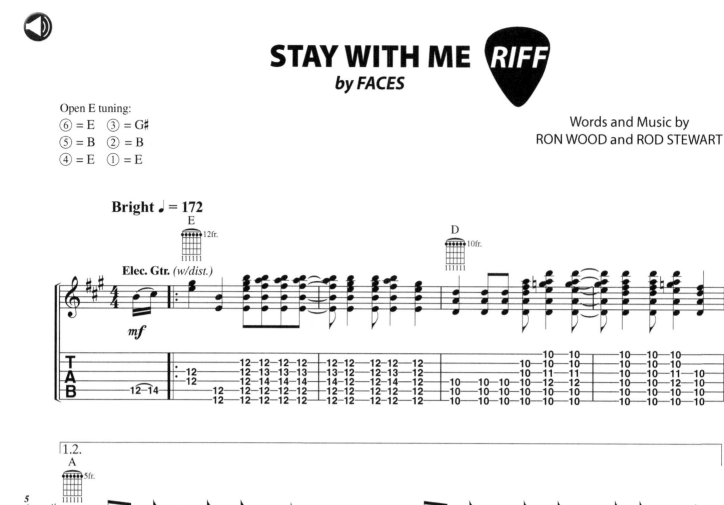

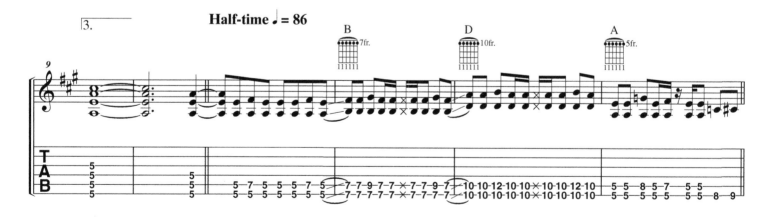

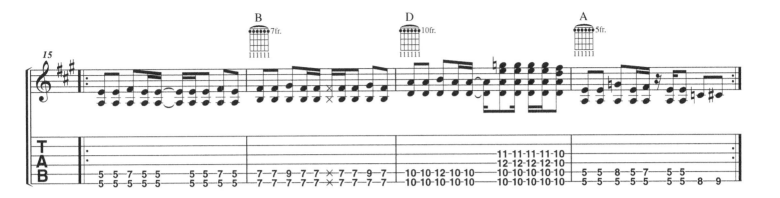

Ron Wood and Rod Stewart created Faces first Top 20 hit, "Stay with Me" in 1972 and its unbridled sass may rival anything created by Wood's future band—the Rolling Stones.

Played in Open E tuning, it starts with a rapid boogie riff but be prepared to slam on the brakes into a half-time groove in measure 9. A humbucker-equipped solidbody guitar and a distortion pedal will probably help you to reproduce the crunchy tone heard on the original record.

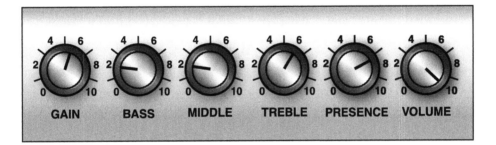

STAYIN' ALIVE
by BEE GEES

Words and Music by
BARRY GIBB, MAURICE GIBB
and ROBIN GIBB

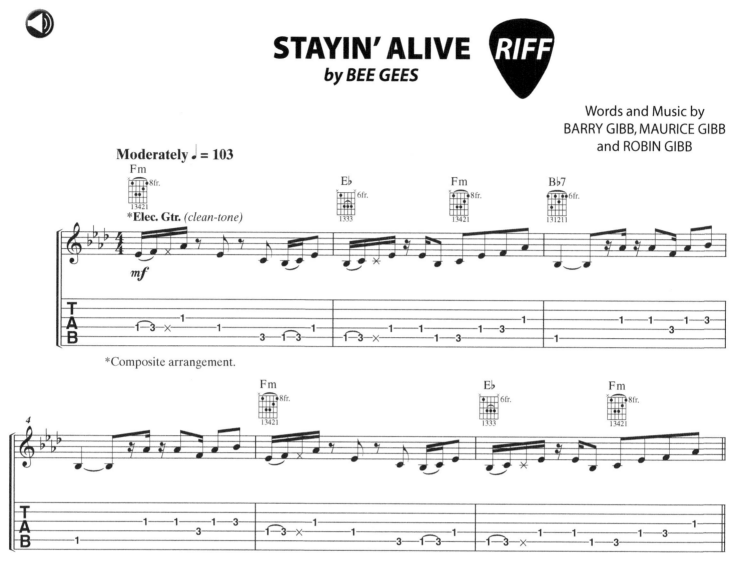

*Composite arrangement.

A Bee Gees chart-topper that will forever be associated with John Travolta strutting down the streets of Brooklyn in the opening scene of the 1977 film *Saturday Night Fever,* "Stayin' Alive" features a catchy R&B guitar riff played by long-time Bee Gees band member Alan Kendall. Like the other funky riffs in this book, keep your picking hand loose and fret the notes somewhat staccato.

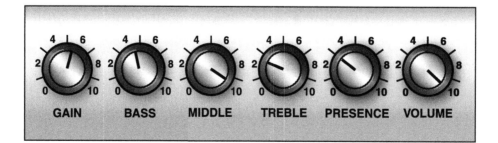

SUMMERTIME BLUES *RIFF*
by THE WHO

Words and Music by
EDDIE COCHRAN and JERRY CAPHEART

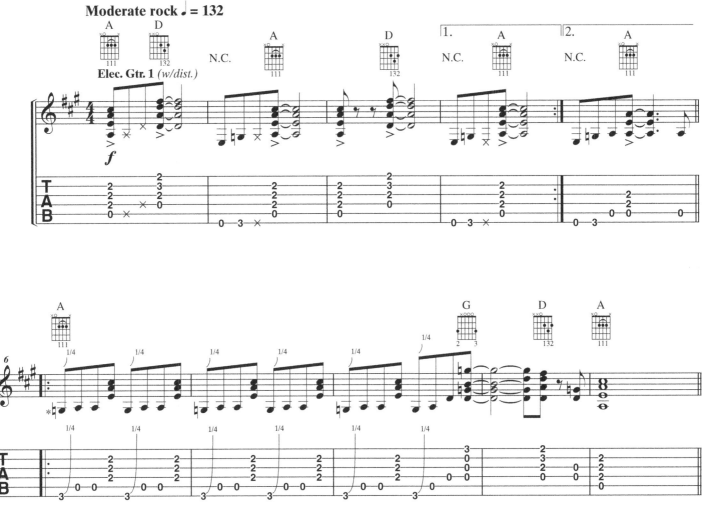

Mod rockers (is that an oxymoron?) the Who ramped up the energy of Eddie Cochran's ode to teen frustration when they tore through this '50s raver.

Guitarist Pete Townshend famously windmilled a P-90-equipped Gibson SG Special through a very loud pair of HiWatt amplifier stacks on the original live recording. The only technical part to watch for in this riff is, starting in measure 6, palm mute the first three single notes before hitting the A chord at the second fret.

SUNSHINE OF YOUR LOVE *RIFF*
by CREAM

Words and Music by
JACK BRUCE, PETE BROWN
and ERIC CLAPTON

Moderately ♩ = 114
Intro:

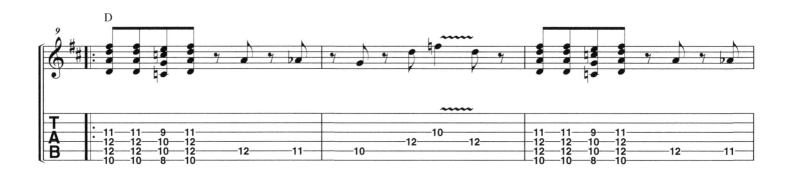

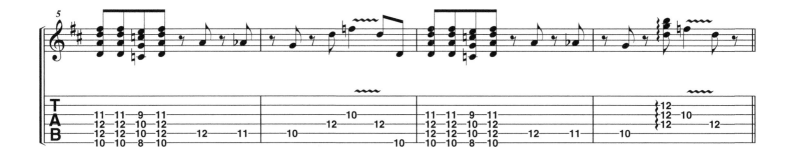

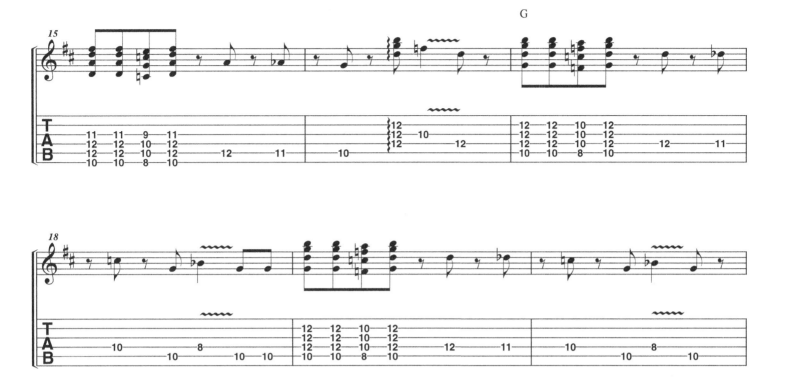

"Sunshine of Your Love" is the best-known song by '60s blues/rock supergroup Cream. Bassist Jack Bruce created the riff and guitarist Eric Clapton embellished it with subtle variations. Notice how the line is basically a descending figure on the first two iterations but, on the third time, Clapton jumps an octave for the last three notes.

For the recording, Clapton used his 1964 Gibson SG into a Marshall tube amplifier.

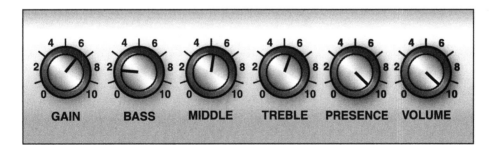

THANK YOU
(FALETTINME BE MICE ELF AGIN)
by SLY & THE FAMILY STONE

Words and Music by
SYLVESTER STEWART

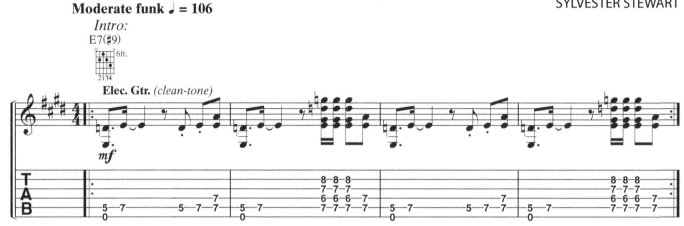

Sly & the Family Stone's "Thank You (Falettinme Be Mice Elf Agin)" is mainly known for introducing Larry Graham's revolutionary slap bass technique but Freddie Stone's equally funky guitar part is also noteworthy. Check it out.

WHOLE LOTTA LOVE
by LED ZEPPELIN

Words and Music by
JIMMY PAGE, ROBERT PLANT,
JOHN PAUL JONES, JOHN BONHAM
and WILLIE DIXON

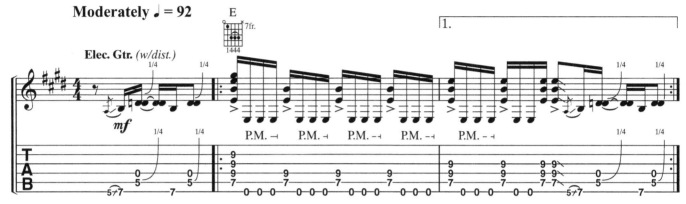

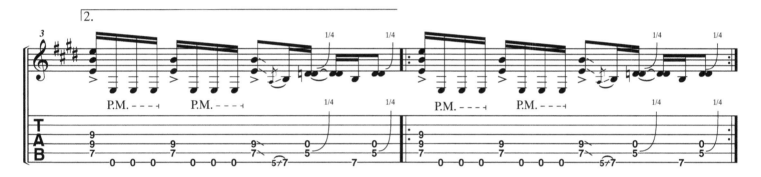

"Whole Lotta Love" kicks off Led Zeppelin's second album in an orgasmic frenzy of blues shouting, thunderous bass and drums, and "The Riff." Jimmy Page's driving guitar part was recorded using a Fender Telecaster into a Marshall "Plexi" amplifier. Part of the drive is from Page's relentless downstrokes punctuated by surprising dissonance of the unison D notes (open 4th string and 5th fret of the 5th string) deliberately bent slightly out of tune from each other.

WHIPPING POST *RIFF*
by THE ALLMAN BROTHERS BAND

Words and Music by
GREGG ALLMAN

Tempo ♪ = 106

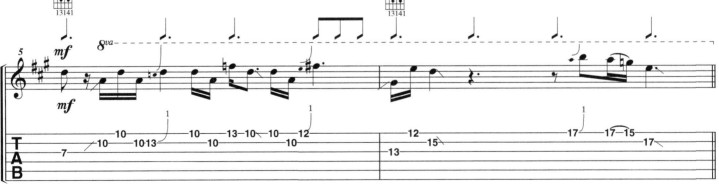

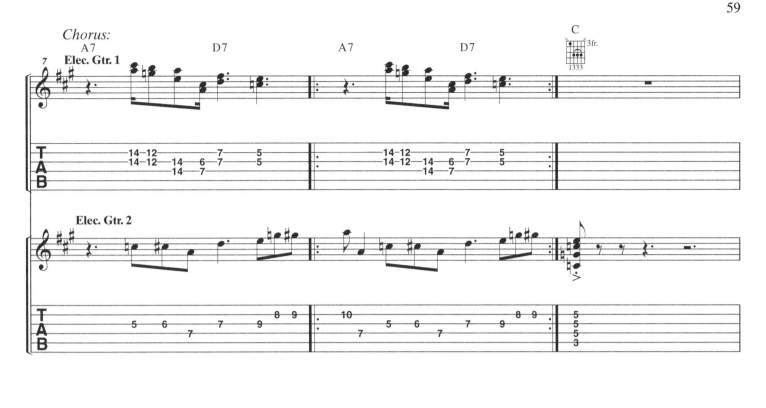

*Divisi: Elec. Gtr. 1 plays upper notes/upper string in TAB,

"Whipping Post' was first recorded by the Allman Brothers Band on their 1969 debut album but it was the outstanding live 23-minute version on *At Fillmore East* (1971) that established Gregg Allman's song as a blues/rock classic. Most of the song is in 12/8 with a solid "three feel" but it's the distinctive intro in 11/8 that draws in the listener. To count the intro, think 1-2-3, 1-2-3, 1-2-3, 1-2.

Elec. Gtr. 1

Elec. Gtr. 2

WILD NIGHT
by VAN MORRISON

Words and Music by
VAN MORRISON

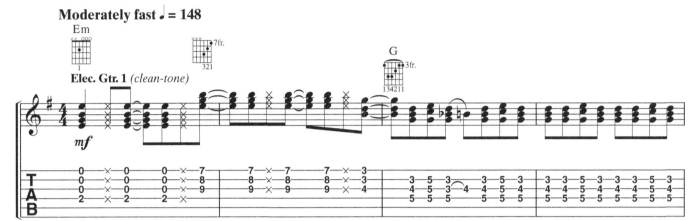

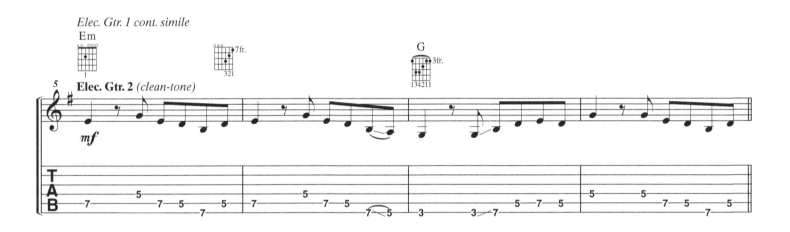

The guitar parts in Van Morrison's "Wild Night" includes both key chordal techniques and key single-note techniques. In the first two measures, note how the muted strings occur on beats 2 and 4. These are the same beats the snare drum customarily emphasizes in a conventional backbeat rhythm. The pattern on the G chord in measures 3 and 4 is classic R&B comping with both embellishments to the IV chord [C] and the hammer-on from a flat 3rd (B♭) to the 3rd (B). The single-note line in measures 5 through 8 is a "guitarist" melodic and rhythmic treatment of a basic E minor (G major) pentatonic scale. Kudos to guitarist Ronnie Montrose for his contributions to Van the Man's original recording.

Elec. Gtr. 1

Elec. Gtr. 2

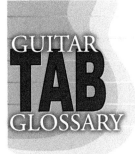

TABLATURE EXPLANATION

TAB illustrates the six strings of the guitar.
Notes and chords are indicated by the placement of fret numbers on each string.

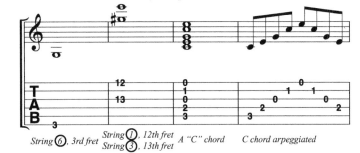

String ⑥, 3rd fret   String ①, 12th fret   A "C" chord   C chord arpeggiated
                      String ③, 13th fret

BENDING NOTES

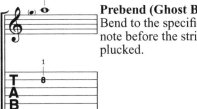

Half Step:
Play the note and bend string one half step (one fret).

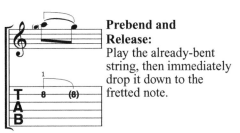

Whole Step:
Play the note and bend string one whole step (two frets).

Slight Bend/ Quarter-Tone Bend:
Play the note and bend string sharp.

Prebend (Ghost Bend):
Bend to the specified note before the string is plucked.

Prebend and Release:
Play the already-bent string, then immediately drop it down to the fretted note.

Unison Bend:
Play both notes and immediately bend the lower note to the same pitch as the higher note.

Bend and Release:
Play the note and bend to the next pitch, then release to the original note. Only the first note is attacked.

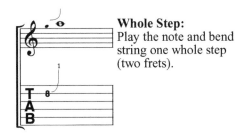

Bends Involving More Than One String:
Play the note and bend the string while playing an additional note on another string. Upon release, relieve the pressure from the additional note allowing the original note to sound alone.

Bends Involving Stationary Notes:
Play both notes and immediately bend the lower note up to pitch. Release bend as indicated.

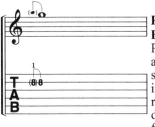

Reverse Bend:
Play the already bent string, then immediately release to drop pitch to fretted note.

Unison Bend:
Play both notes and immediately bend the lower note to the same pitch as the higher note.

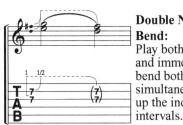

Double Note Bend:
Play both notes and immediately bend both strings simultaneously up the indicated intervals.

ARTICULATIONS

Hammer On (Ascending Slur): Play the lower note, then "hammer" your finger to the higher note. Only the first note is plucked.

Pull Off (Descending Slur): Play the higher note with your first finger already in position on the lower note. Pull your finger off the first note with a strong downward motion that plucks the string—sounding the lower note.

Legato Slide: Play the first note and, keeping pressure applied on the string, slide up to the second note. The diagonal line shows that it is a slide and not a hammer-on or a pull-off.

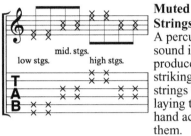

Muted Strings: A percussive sound is produced by striking the strings while laying the fret hand across them.

Palm Mute: The notes are muted (muffled) by placing the palm of the pick hand lightly on the strings, just in front of the bridge.

Left Hand Hammer: Using only the left hand, hammer on the first note played on each string.

Glissando: Play note and slide in specified direction.

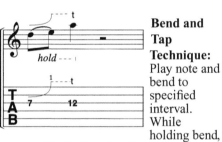

Bend and Tap Technique: Play note and bend to specified interval. While holding bend, tap onto fret indicated with a "t."

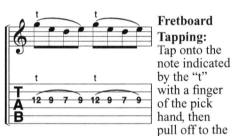

Fretboard Tapping: Tap onto the note indicated by the "t" with a finger of the pick hand, then pull off to the following note held by the fret hand.

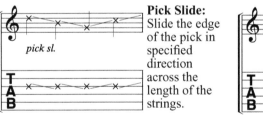

Pick Slide: Slide the edge of the pick in specified direction across the length of the strings.

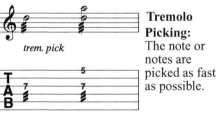

Tremolo Picking: The note or notes are picked as fast as possible.

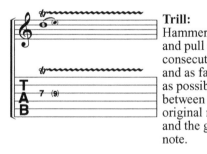

Trill: Hammer on and pull off consecutively and as fast as possible between the original note and the grace note.

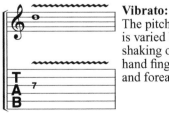

Vibrato: The pitch of a note is varied by a rapid shaking of the fret-hand finger, wrist, and forearm.

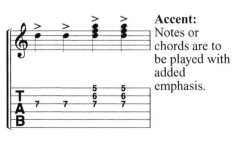

Accent: Notes or chords are to be played with added emphasis.

Staccato (Detached Notes): Notes or chords are to be played about half their noted value and with separation.

HARMONICS

Natural Harmonic:
A finger of the fret hand lightly touches the string at the note indicated in the TAB and is plucked by the pick producing a bell-like sound called a harmonic.

Artificial Harmonic:
Fret the note at the first TAB number, lightly touch the string at the fret indicated in parens (usually 12 frets higher than the fretted note), then pluck the string with an available finger or your pick.

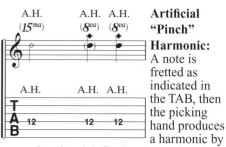

Artificial "Pinch" Harmonic:
A note is fretted as indicated in the TAB, then the picking hand produces a harmonic by squeezing the pick firmly while using the tip of the index finger in the pick attack. If parenthesis are found around the fretted note, it does not sound. No parenthesis means both the fretted note and the A.H. are heard simultaneously.

RHYTHM SLASHES

Strum Marks/ Rhythm Slashes:
Strum with the indicated rhythm pattern. Strum marks can be located above the staff or within the staff.

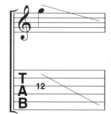

Single Notes with Rhythm Slashes:
Sometimes single notes are incorporated into a strum pattern. The circled number below is the string and the fret number is above.

TREMOLO BAR

Specified Interval:
The pitch of a note or chord is lowered to the specified interval and then return as indicated. The action of the tremolo bar is graphically represented by the peaks and valleys of the diagram.

Unspecified Interval:
The pitch of a note or chord is lowered, usually very dramatically, until the pitch of the string becomes indeterminate.

PICK DIRECTION

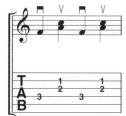

Downstrokes and Upstrokes:
The downstroke is indicated with this symbol (⊓) and the upstroke is indicated with this (V).